P9-CKS-668

States

KENTUCKY

by Angie Swanson

CAPSTONE PRESS
a capstone imprint

Next Page Books are published by Capstone Press,
1710 Roe Crest Drive, North Mankato, Minnesota 56003
www.mycapstone.com

Library of Congress Cataloging-in-Publication Data
Cataloging-in-publication information is on file with the Library of
Congress.
ISBN 978-1-5157-0404-1 (library binding)
ISBN 978-1-5157-0463-8 (paperback)
ISBN 978-1-5157-0515-4 (ebook PDF)

Editorial Credits
Jaclyn Jaycox, editor; Kazuko Collins and Katy LaVigne, designers;
Morgan Walters, media researcher; Laura Manthe, production specialist

Photo Credits
Alamy: North Wind Picture Archives, 25; Capstone Press: Angi Gahler,
map 4, 7; CriaImages.com/Jay Robert Nash Collection, middle 18,
bottom 19; Dreamstime: Erica Schroeder, 11, Michael Wood, bottom
left 21, Muchak, 9; Getty Images: Mike Simons, 29, PhotoQuest, 12,
Underwood Archives, 28; Library of Congress: Prints and Photographs
Division Washington, D.C, 27; One Mile Up, Inc., flag, seal 23;
Shutterstock: Alexey Stiop, bottom left 8, Andriy Solovyov, bottom 24,
Anne Kitzman, bottom right 8, 10, ashkabe, 14, Cheryl Ann Quigley,
bottom right 20, Connie Barr, bottom left 20, cristalvi, top left 20,
Darren Brode, 15, Elena Elisseeva, top right 20, Erni, top right 21,
Everett Historical, 26, Featureflash, top 18, top 19, goldenjack, cover,
jessicakirsh, 17, Lynn Watson, middle left 21, Madlen, middle right
21, Michael Shake, 6, Neale Cousland, 16, Neveshkin Nikolay, bottom
18, Phent, 7, Praiwun Thungsarn, top 24, s_bukley, middle 19, Sari
ONeal, bottom right 21, Sementer, top left 21, Steven Frame, 13, Todd
Taulman, 5

All design elements by Shutterstock

Printed and bound in China.
0316/CA21600187
012016   009436F16

TABLE OF CONTENTS

Want to take your research further? Ask your librarian if your school subscribes to PebbleGo Next. If so, when you see this helpful symbol 🖱 throughout the book, log onto www.pebblegonext.com for bonus downloads and information.

LOCATION

Kentucky is in the east-central United States. Indiana and Ohio are to the north. West Virginia and Virginia share Kentucky's eastern border. Tennessee lies to the south. Missouri and Illinois are west of Kentucky. The capital, Frankfort, lies along the Kentucky River, which flows north from the Appalachian Mountains through the eastern part of the state. The state's largest cities are Louisville, Lexington, and Bowling Green.

PebbleGo Next Bonus! To print and label your own map, go to www.pebblegonext.com and search keywords: **KY MAP**

Kentucky's second-largest city, Louisville, is a major river port for the state.

GEOGRAPHY

Eastern Kentucky has many high ridges and narrow valleys and includes the Appalachian Plateau. Forests cover much of this region. The Cumberland and Pine mountains are in this area. Black Mountain, the highest point in Kentucky, is part of the Cumberland Mountains. It rises 4,139 feet (1,262 meters) above sea level.

PebbleGo Next Bonus! To watch a video about the Louisville Slugger factory, go to www.pebblegonext.com and search keywords: **KY VIDEO**

In north-central Kentucky, the Bluegrass Region has many rolling hills. The Mississippi Plateau takes up much of south-central and southwestern Kentucky. Kentucky's richest farmland is found in this area. Many caves lie beneath the Mississippi Plateau. Northwestern Kentucky is hilly and has large coal deposits. The Jackson Purchase is the southwestern tip of Kentucky.

Cumberland Falls, located in southeastern Kentucky, is a popular tourist attraction.

The Appalachian Plateau area overlooks forests and mountains.

Ohio River
BLUEGRASS REGION
Big Sandy River
Kentucky River
APPALACHIAN PLATEAU
Mississippi River
WESTERN COALFIELD
Mammoth Cave National Park
Lake Cumberland
Green River
Black Mountain
Lake Barkley
MISSISSIPPI PLATEAU
PINE MOUNTAINS
JACKSON PURCHASE
Cumberland River
Cumberland Gap National Historical Park
CUMBERLAND MOUNTAINS
Kentucky Lake
Tennessee River

Legend
▲ Highest Point
Lake
National Park
River

Scale
Miles
0 25 50 75 100
0 25 50 75 100
Kilometers

WEATHER

Kentuckians enjoy mild weather throughout the year. Summers are generally warm. The average summer temperature is 75 degrees Fahrenheit (24 degrees Celsius). Winters are cool but not very cold. The average winter temperature is 36°F (2°C).

Average High and Low Temperatures (Frankfort, KY)

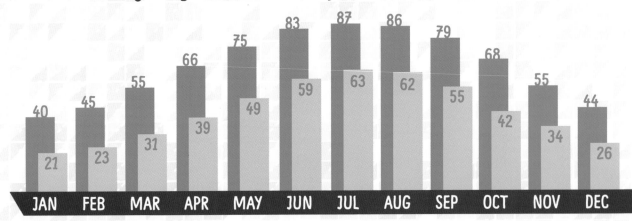

Month	High	Low
JAN	40	21
FEB	45	23
MAR	55	31
APR	66	39
MAY	75	49
JUN	83	59
JUL	87	63
AUG	86	62
SEP	79	55
OCT	68	42
NOV	55	34
DEC	44	26

LANDMARKS

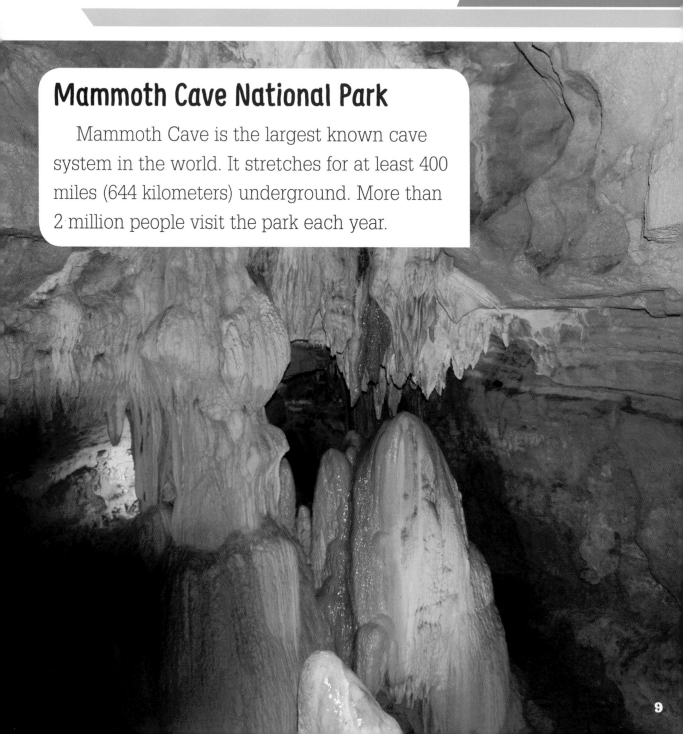

Mammoth Cave National Park

Mammoth Cave is the largest known cave system in the world. It stretches for at least 400 miles (644 kilometers) underground. More than 2 million people visit the park each year.

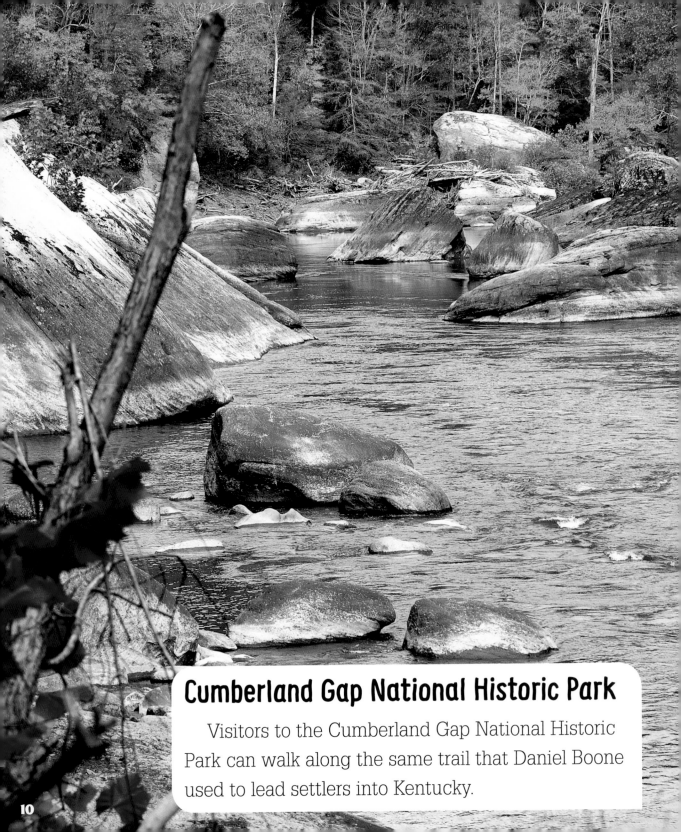

Cumberland Gap National Historic Park

Visitors to the Cumberland Gap National Historic Park can walk along the same trail that Daniel Boone used to lead settlers into Kentucky.

Kentucky Derby Museum

The Kentucky Derby Museum at Churchill Downs in Louisville gives visitors a look at this famous horse racetrack. Visitors can see the track, the fancy places where the wealthy watch the race, and exhibits about the history of this famous race.

The Wilderness Road served as the passageway to Kentucky for about 300,000 settlers.

In 1750 explorer Thomas Walker found an American Indian path through the Appalachian Mountains. He named it the Cumberland Gap. Pioneer Daniel Boone led many groups of settlers across the Cumberland Gap and into Kentucky. The trail became known as the Wilderness Road. During the Revolutionary War (1775–1783), many American Indians helped the British. In 1778 Daniel Boone led a successful defense of Boonesborough. After the colonists won their freedom, thousands of settlers moved west to Kentucky. In 1792 Kentucky became the 15th state. Kentucky was the first state west of the Appalachian Mountains.

Kentucky's government is divided into three branches. The executive branch, led by the governor, carries out laws. The legislative branch makes state laws. The General Assembly is divided into the 38-member Senate and the 100-member House of Representatives. Kentucky's judges and courts make up the judicial branch. It upholds the laws.

Kentucky's legislative bodies meet in the House and Sentate chambers.

INDUSTRY

Agriculture decreased in importance in Kentucky after World War II. But tobacco is still a major crop. Other crops grown in the state include corn, soybeans, and wheat. Farmers in Kentucky also raise livestock, including cattle, chickens, hogs, and sheep. The Bluegrass Region is famous for thoroughbred horses. These fast horses are bred for racing.

Cars and trucks are Kentucky's leading manufactured products. In 1988 Toyota opened its first plant in the United States in Georgetown. Chevrolet's Corvette sports cars are manufactured in Bowling Green. Ford builds trucks in Louisville. Other factories in Kentucky produce home appliances and tobacco products.

There are about 450 thoroughbred horse farms in Kentucky.

Coal is Kentucky's most important mining product. Coal deposits lie under 40 percent of Kentucky's land. Oil, natural gas, limestone, and clay are other natural resources mined in Kentucky.

About 50,000 tourists from around the world visit the Corvette assembly plant in Bowling Green each year.

POPULATION

Most Kentuckians come from European backgrounds. About 86 percent of the people in Kentucky are white. Many of these people have English, Scottish, or German backgrounds.

African-Americans are the state's next largest ethnic group. This population includes descendants of former slaves. Kentucky's Hispanic population more than doubled from 2000 to 2010. Asian Americans make up about 1 percent of the state's population. They moved to Kentucky from China, India, and the Philippines. Kentucky's small American Indian population descended from Cherokee, Shawnee, and Creek Indians.

Population by Ethnicity

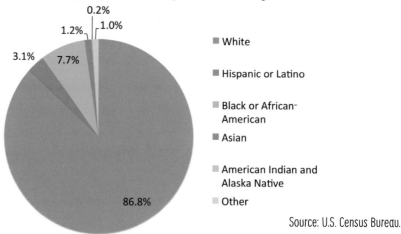

- White
- Hispanic or Latino
- Black or African-American
- Asian
- American Indian and Alaska Native
- Other

0.2%
1.2%
1.0%
3.1%
7.7%
86.8%

Source: U.S. Census Bureau.

Over 170,000 people attended the 141st Kentucky Derby in 2015.

FAMOUS PEOPLE

Muhammad Ali (1942–) was a world champion boxer. After retiring from boxing, Ali worked with many charities. He was born as Cassius Clay in Louisville.

Jefferson Davis (1808–1889) was president of the Confederate States of America during the Civil War. He was born in Christian (now Todd) County.

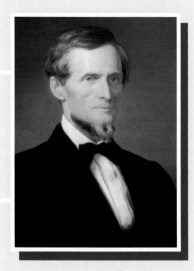

Abraham Lincoln (1809–1865) was the 16th U.S. president. He was born in Hardin County. He led the United States during the Civil War and was shot and killed by John Wilkes Booth in 1865.

Johnny Depp (1963–) was born in Owensboro. He has starred in many popular movies, such as the *Pirates of the Caribbean* movies.

Jennifer Lawrence (1990–) is an Academy Award–winning actress. Born in Louisville, she is best known for her role as Katniss Everdeen in *The Hunger Games* movies.

Daniel Boone (1734–1820) was an explorer and frontiersman. Born in Pennsylvania, he founded the town of Boonesborough, Kentucky.

STATE SYMBOLS

tulip poplar
Tree

goldenrod
Flower

Kentucky cardinal
Bird

thoroughbred
Horse

PebbleGo Next Bonus! To make a "Kentucky Derby" pie, go to www.pebblegonext.com and search keywords:

KY RECIPE

Fossil

brachiopod

Animal

gray squirrel

Music

bluegrass music

Rock

Kentucky agate

Fish

Kentucky bass

Butterfly

viceroy

21

FAST FACTS

STATEHOOD
1792

CAPITAL ☆
Frankfort

LARGEST CITY •
Louisville

SIZE
39,486 square miles (102,268 square kilometers)
land area (2010 U.S. Census Bureau)

POPULATION
4,395,295 (2013 U.S. Census estimate)

STATE NICKNAME
The Bluegrass State

STATE MOTTO
"United we stand, divided we fall"

STATE SEAL

A pioneer shakes hands with a statesman in the middle of Kentucky's state seal. The pioneer represents Kentucky's frontier settlers. The statesman represents Kentuckians who served in state and federal government. The state motto, "United we stand, divided we fall," circles the two figures. The motto comes from "Liberty Song," by John Dickinson. Across the top of the seal is written "Commonwealth of Kentucky," the official state name. The flowers across the bottom of the seal are goldenrod, the state flower.

PebbleGo Next Bonus!
To print and color your own flag, go to www.pebblegonext.com and search keywords:
KY FLAG

STATE FLAG

Kentucky's state flag features the state seal in the middle of a navy blue background. Across the top of the seal is written "Commonwealth of Kentucky," the official state name. A pioneer shakes hands with a statesman in the middle of Kentucky's state seal. The pioneer represents Kentucky's frontier settlers. The statesman represents Kentuckians who served in state and federal government. Their handshake represents the state motto, which appears on the flag, "United we stand, divided we fall."

MINING PRODUCTS

coal, natural gas, limestone, clay

MANUFACTURED GOODS

tobacco products, motor vehicle parts, chemicals, machinery, metal products, petroleum and coal products

FARM PRODUCTS

tobacco, corn, soybeans, wheat, horses, cattle

PebbleGo Next Bonus!
To learn the lyrics to
the state song, go to
www.pebblegonext.com
and search keywords:
KY SONG

KENTUCKY TIMELINE

1620 — The Pilgrims establish a colony in the New World in present-day Massachusetts.

1654 — Abraham Wood makes the first recorded trip to Kentucky. At the time, Cherokee, Chickasaw, Shawnee, Creek, and Mingo Indians live and hunt in the area.

1750 — Thomas Walker enters Kentucky through the Cumberland Gap.

1774 — James Harrod founds Harrodstown, Kentucky's first permanent white settlement.

1775 — Pioneer Daniel Boone helps found Boonesborough.

1778

During the Revolutionary War Daniel Boone leads a successful defense of Boonesborough against American Indians who were fighting for the British.

1792

Kentucky becomes the 15th state on June 1.

1809

On February 12 Abraham Lincoln is born in a cabin near Hodgenville, Kentucky.

1818

General Andrew Jackson negotiates a land purchase from the Chickasaw Indians. Called the Jackson Purchase, the deal expands Kentucky's borders.

1861–1865

The Union and the Confederacy fight the Civil War. Kentucky declares itself neutral, but Kentuckians fight for both the Union and the Confederacy.

1875 The first Kentucky Derby is run on May 17 at Churchill Downs. This race is the oldest continually run horse race in the United States.

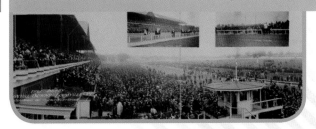

EARLY 1900s Coal mines open in eastern and western Kentucky.

1904 Tobacco companies lower the prices they pay tobacco farmers. The farmers fight back against the companies' low prices in what becomes known as the Black Patch War.

1914–1918 World War I is fought; the United States enters the war in 1917.

1926 Mammoth Cave National Park is established.

1933
The Tennessee Valley Authority begins building dams in Kentucky.

1936
The U.S. government begins storing gold at Fort Knox.

1966
Kentucky lawmakers pass the Kentucky Civil Rights Act. This law requires that all people receive equal chances for employment and housing. Kentucky is the first southern state to pass a civil rights law.

1970
On December 30, 38 coal miners are killed in an explosion in Hyden.

1978
Congress passes a law requiring coal mine owners to repair the land they mine.

1988 Japanese auto manufacturer Toyota opens its first U.S. plant in Georgetown.

1990 Kentucky's legislature passes the Kentucky Education Reform Act. This law provides money to train teachers, purchase school equipment, and create more preschool classes.

2000 On October 11 a coal waste spill pollutes eastern Kentucky rivers and streams.

2012 On March 2 and 3 a tornado outbreak over several southern states kills 22 people in Kentucky.

2015 Jenean Hampton becomes the first African-American to be elected to statewide office in Kentucky.

Glossary

ethnicity *(ETH-niss-ih-tee)*—a group of people who share the same physical features, beliefs, and backgrounds

executive *(ig-ZE-kyuh-tiv)*—the branch of government that makes sure laws are followed

frontier *(fruhn-TIHR)*—the far edge of a settled area, where few people live

industry *(IN-duh-stree)*—a business which produces a product or provides a service

legislature *(LEJ-iss-lay-chur)*—a group of elected officials who have the power to make or change laws for a country or state

limestone *(LIME-stohn)*—hard rock used in building; made from the remains of ancient sea creatures

petroleum *(puh-TROH-lee-uhm)*—an oily liquid found below the earth's surface used to make gasoline, heating oil, and many other products

plateau *(pla-TOH)*—an area of high, flat land

region *(REE-juhn)*—a large area

sea level *(SEE LEV-uhl)*—the average level of the surface of the ocean, used as a starting point from which to measure the height or depth of any place

Read More

Edgar, Sherra G. *What's Great About Kentucky?* Our Great States. Minneapolis: Lerner Publications, 2016.

Gaines, Ann. *Kentucky.* It's My State! New York: Cavendish Square Publishing, 2017.

Ganeri, Anita. *United States of America: A Benjamin Blog and His Inquisitive Dog Guide.* Country Guides. Chicago: Heinemann Raintree, 2015.

Internet Sites

FactHound offers a safe, fun way to find Internet sites related to this book. All of the sites on FactHound have been researched by our staff.

Here's all you do:

Visit *www.facthound.com*

Type in this code: 9781515704041

Super-cool stuff! Check out projects, games and lots more at **www.capstonekids.com**

Critical Thinking Using the Common Core

1. What is the state tree of Kentucky? (Key Ideas and Details)

2. Kentucky is the first state west of the Appalachian Mountains. If you were a pioneer traveling west, what features of Kentucky might have made you stay instead of moving farther west? (Integration of Knowledge and Ideas)

3. What percentage of Kentucky's population is Black or African-American? For help, use the pie graph on page 16. (Craft and Structure)

Index

31901062696366